Meerkats

Victoria Blakemore

Copyright info/picture credits

Cover, NischAporn/AdobeStock; Page 3, Mojpe/Pixabay; Page 5, Alexas_Fotos/Pixabay; Page 7, TLSPAMG/Pixabay; Page 9, Maciej Czekajewski/AdobeStock; Pages 10-11, Iuliia Sokolovska/AdobeStock; Page 13, LyraBelacqua-Sally/Pixabay; Page 15, jay-clarke1/Pixabay; Page 17, JakeWilliamHeckey/Pixabay; Page 19, Alexas_Fotos/Pixabay; Page 21, Co_Sch/Pixabay; Page 23, Mike1087/Pixabay; Page 25; NischAporn/AdobeStock; Page 27, bed-nuts/Pixabay; Page 29, CountryGirl1/Pixabay; Page 31, Bohun_pl/Pixabay; Page 33, skeeze/Pixabay; Page 35, Hazi54/Pixabay

Table of Contents

What Are Meerkats?

Meerkats are small mammals that are members of the mongoose family.

Their fur is many shades of brown, orange, and gray. It works as **camouflage** and helps them to blend in to the dirt.

Size

Adult meerkats can grow to be about 10 inches in length. Their long tail adds up to eight more inches.

Adult meerkats usually weigh less than two pounds. That is about the same weight as a squirrel.

Male meerkats are usually

longer and heavier than

female meerkats.

Physical Characteristics

Meerkats have long paws with sharp claws. They use their claws to dig burrows in the dirt.

Meerkats have a long tail. It helps meerkats to balance when they are standing up.

Meerkats have dark fur around their eyes. It helps them see in the bright sunlight.

Habitat

Meerkats live in deserts, plains, and savannas. The land is mainly flat and is mostly sand or dirt.

The dirt in their habitat is soft. It is easy for meerkats to dig burrows in.

Range

Meerkats are only found on the continent of Africa.

They are found in the southern parts of Africa. This includes the Kalahari desert.

II

Diet

Meerkats are **omnivores**, which means that they eat meat and plants.

They eat insects, lizards, birds, and fruit. Meerkats work together to **forage** for food.

Meerkats may dig in the dirt to

look for insects to eat.

Some meerkats act as lookouts and watch for **predators**, such as eagles or jackals. Others forage for food.

If they spot a predator, meerkats have a very shrill call that they make to warn each other of danger.

Meerkats often stand on

their **hind legs** so they can

see farther. 15

Communication

Meerkats use mainly scent and sound to communicate. They may mark their **territory** with special scent glands on their cheeks and under their tail.

Meerkats make sounds such as barks, shrill calls, and cries.

Many meerkat sounds are used to warn others of danger.

Movement

When meerkats run, they run on all four legs. This helps them to run very fast. They have been known to run up to twenty miles per hour.

When meerkats run, they look very similar to cats.

Meerkats are also able to climb rocks and trees to look for predators.

Warming Up

Meerkats have a patch on their stomach where the hair is very thin. This allows their black skin to be seen.

When meerkats stand on their hind legs, the sun hits this spot. Their skin **absorbs** the heat and they warm up.

When meerkats come out of

their burrows in the morning,

they need to warm up.

Mob Life

Meerkats are very social animals. They spend most of their time together.

They live in groups that are called "mobs." Each mob is a family group that is made up of up to forty meerkats.

Meerkats hunt, groom, and play together.

Burrows

Meerkats live in burrows that they dig in the dirt. Mobs have several burrows that they live in at different times.

Burrows have many holes called bolt holes. Meerkats use them if they need to escape a predator quickly.

Burrows also keep meerkats cool

in the day and warm at night.

Meerkat Pups

Meerkats usually have between two and four pups. When they are first born, pups can't see or hear, and they are almost hairless.

Meerkats take turns watching the pups so that the parents can look for food.

Meerkat pups will be able to

help forage by the time they

are about ten months old.

Life Span

In the wild, meerkats often live between six and ten years. In **captivity**, meerkats can live up to fourteen years.

The difference is that meerkats in captivity have enough food. They also don't have any predators.

Population

Meerkats are listed as low risk. There are many still left in the wild. They are not in danger of **extinction** at this time.

Researchers believe that there are over 500,000 meerkats living in the wild.

Even though they are not

endangered, meerkats still face

threats in the wild.

Meerkats are sometimes hunted because they can carry diseases.

Their habitat can be destroyed if people build roads and buildings.

There are groups like the

Meerkat Magic Conservation

Project who are working to

help meerkats.

They help to **preserve** land.

They want to keep people

from destroying meerkats

habitats.

Glossary

Absorb: to take in or soak up

Camouflage: using color to blend in to the surroundings

Captivity: when animals are kept by people, not in the wild

Endangered: at risk of becoming extinct

Extinction: when there are no more of an animal left alive

Forage: search for food

Hind Legs: the back legs of an animal

Omnivore: an animal that eats meat and plants

Predators: animals that hunt and eat other animals

Preserve: to protect from being harmed

Territory: an area of land that an animal claims as its own

About the Author

Victoria Blakemore is a first grade

teacher in Southwest Florida with a

passion for reading.

You can visit her at

www.elementaryexplorers.com

Also in This Series

Elementary Explorers **Gray Wolves** Victoria Blakemore	Elementary Explorers **Sloths** Victoria Blakemore	Elementary Explorers **Flamingos** Victoria Blakemore	Elementary Explorers **Camels** Victoria Blakemore	Elementary Explorers **Koalas** Victoria Blakemore	Elementary Explorers **Honey Bees** Victoria Blakemore
Elementary Explorers **Pandas** Victoria Blakemore	Elementary Explorers **Pangolins** Victoria Blakemore	Elementary Explorers **White-Tailed Deer** Victoria Blakemore	Elementary Explorers **Orcas** Victoria Blakemore	Elementary Explorers **Giraffes** Victoria Blakemore	Elementary Explorers **Corn** Victoria Blakemore
Elementary Explorers **Meerkats** Victoria Blakemore	Elementary Explorers **Echidnas** Victoria Blakemore	Elementary Explorers **Walruses** Victoria Blakemore	Elementary Explorers **Raccoons** Victoria Blakemore	Elementary Explorers **Bald Eagles** Victoria Blakemore	Elementary Explorers **Apples** Victoria Blakemore
Elementary Explorers **Arctic Foxes** Victoria Blakemore	Elementary Explorers **Red Pandas** Victoria Blakemore	Elementary Explorers **Cassowaries** Victoria Blakemore	Elementary Explorers **Tigers** Victoria Blakemore	Elementary Explorers **Ladybugs** Victoria Blakemore	Elementary Explorers **Moose** Victoria Blakemore
Elementary Explorers **Beluga Whales** Victoria Blakemore	Elementary Explorers **Leopards** Victoria Blakemore	Elementary Explorers **Elephants** Victoria Blakemore	Elementary Explorers **Jellyfish** Victoria Blakemore	Elementary Explorers **Binturongs** Victoria Blakemore	Elementary Explorers **Lions** Victoria Blakemore
Elementary Explorers **Dolphins** Victoria Blakemore	Elementary Explorers **Reindeer** Victoria Blakemore	Elementary Explorers **Hammerhead Sharks** Victoria Blakemore	Elementary Explorers **Hippos** Victoria Blakemore	Elementary Explorers **Pumpkins** Victoria Blakemore	Elementary Explorers **Peafowl** Victoria Blakemore

Also in This Series

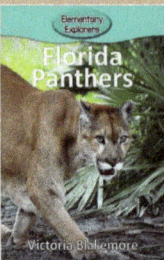

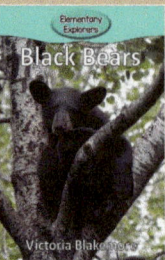

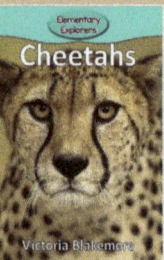

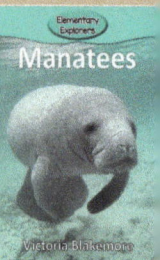

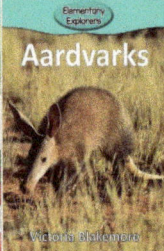

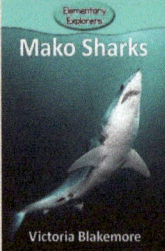

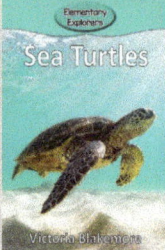

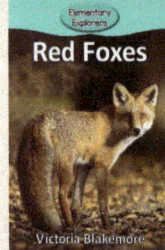

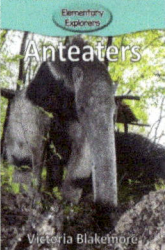

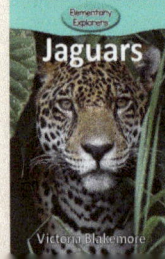

Elementary Explorers — Chameleons — Victoria Blakemore

Elementary Explorers — Florida Panthers — Victoria Blakemore

Elementary Explorers — Aye-Ayes — Victoria Blakemore

Elementary Explorers — Black Bears — Victoria Blakemore

Elementary Explorers — Cheetahs — Victoria Blakemore

Elementary Explorers — Manatees — Victoria Blakemore

Elementary Explorers — Gingerbread — Victoria Blakemore

Elementary Explorers — Polar Bears — Victoria Blakemore

Elementary Explorers — Hot Chocolate — Victoria Blakemore

Elementary Explorers — Orangutans — Victoria Blakemore

Elementary Explorers — Coyotes — Victoria Blakemore

Elementary Explorers — Marshmallows — Victoria Blakemore

Elementary Explorers — Strawberries — Victoria Blakemore

Elementary Explorers — Aardvarks — Victoria Blakemore

Elementary Explorers — Mako Sharks — Victoria Blakemore

Elementary Explorers — Alligators — Victoria Blakemore

Elementary Explorers — Frogs — Victoria Blakemore

Elementary Explorers — Hedgehogs — Victoria Blakemore

Elementary Explorers — Brown Bears — Victoria Blakemore

Elementary Explorers — Bongos — Victoria Blakemore

Elementary Explorers — Sea Turtles — Victoria Blakemore

Elementary Explorers — Quokkas — Victoria Blakemore

Elementary Explorers — Muskrats — Victoria Blakemore

Elementary Explorers — Zebras — Victoria Blakemore

Elementary Explorers — Red Foxes — Victoria Blakemore

Elementary Explorers — Ring-Tailed Lemurs — Victoria Blakemore

Elementary Explorers — Platypuses — Victoria Blakemore

Elementary Explorers — Anteaters — Victoria Blakemore

Elementary Explorers — Kangaroos — Victoria Blakemore

Elementary Explorers — Rhinos — Victoria Blakemore

Elementary Explorers — Jaguars — Victoria Blakemore

Elementary Explorers — Wombats — Victoria Blakemore

www.ingramcontent.com/pod-product-compliance
Lightning Source LLC
Chambersburg PA
CBHW051250020426
42333CB00025B/3138